C000085814

8 Kerinsian Keys

to

Self Empowerment

Life Coaching Made Easy

Bill Kerins   Dip. CAH ACPAMT

Disclaimer

This book is intended to teach the basics of Life Coaching for personal and professional use. The techniques are simple and easy to learn. However, you, the reader, must assume responsibility for your own emotional, physical and spiritual welfare. Please use your common sense. If in doubt, it is wise to seek the help of a qualified Life Coach.

The author and publisher disclaim any liability arising directly or indirectly from the use of this book and take no responsibility whatsoever for your actions or the outcome of any treatment administered by you, on yourself or others.

First Edition printed July 2007

Copyright © 2007: Bill Kerins Dip. CAH ACPAMT

Published by
New Vision Media LLP

www.newvisionmedia.co.uk

ISBN 978-0-9549222-4-5

Printed and bound in the UK by T.J. International
Padstow, Cornwall

Acknowledgements

I would like to thank my wife Patricia Iris Kerins for
the encouragement and patience she has given to
this project, and to all my students, teachers and
colleagues who contributed to this book in their
own distinct way.

Contents

Preface

This little book is designed to help you, the reader, to learn and develop some simple everyday techniques, which will help to improve your life and help you to help others.

It is not a dogma or belief system; it is a simple guide.

The benefits of this book are felt by those who are:

- Open minded

- Committed

- Somewhat disciplined

- Eager to learn more about themselves

If you can match some or even **all** of the above, then read on.

By **open minded**, I mean, 'be non-judgemental'. Don't limit your learning by 'poo-hooing' or ridiculing some of these techniques. Be open to look at, try them out and then decide what is right for you.

1

ᴹ

By **committed** I mean, 'go for it'. Read, and then practise these techniques as often as you possibly can. Set yourself a set of goals e.g.

- Certain times of the day / week.

- Remain focussed on the goals.
  For a certain period of time – three / four months.

- Do not be distracted by others.

By **disciplined** I mean, 'do it regularly' – without fail or excuses. Affirm to yourself that you will be disciplined. Set aside times of the day (or week) when you will carry out these exercises. Very soon you will feel the enormous benefits and perhaps surprise yourself.

Self-discipline is 'entraining' the mind and body to perform to it's own unique and outstanding ability.

By **eager to learn** I mean, ' be **willing** to read, process and then decide on how much you want to accept'. As I have said before – this is not a dogma or a faith.

Introduction

Life is one long lesson. The longer we live, the more we learn, and the more we realise that there is even more to learn. It is an ongoing adventure.

I have written this book in such a way that you can open and read it at any chapter. However, I would suggest that you read the entire book.

Nothing is gained by waiting for life to happen. This form of thinking leads to 'victimisation'.

Victimisation is a passive role we play when we are not ready – or refuse to fully participate in the process of our own life.

I hear so many people complaining that their life is boring or compulsory – "I <u>have</u> to do this job". But, what would you do if you had complete choice ??

Imagine that you were in charge of what happens in your life. How different would it be from what it is now ?? What would you be doing ?? Where in the world would you live ??

What is actually preventing you from achieving some – if not <u>all</u> of your dreams ??

I'd be willing to bet that the answer to the last question above would be something like "I have to pay my mortgage" or "I have to look after someone else – other than myself".

I'm not suggesting that you abandon every responsibility in your life and become a monk or a world traveller. But I am suggesting that you take a long hard look at what is going on in your life right now, and start to make a life plan for *you* – not your family – not your business – but for *you*. What is it that you want to achieve as a person ?

The most important person in your life is reading this little book right now - and that's *you*.

When you start to fulfil your dreams and ambitions, the knock-on effect on those around you is profound. It may appear that you are being selfish, but I can assure you that when you serve and honour yourself –- you serve humanity. This includes your family, friends and work colleagues.

Serving yourself in an honest, truthful way is the single most important thing you can do in this lifetime. I'm not talking about selfishness – I'm talking about self-fullness. There is a difference.

Selfishness is an "I'm alright Jack" attitude. Taking more than your share. Thinking only of you in a selfish way.

Self-fullness, on the other hand, is totally respecting and loving you. This kind of person considers others, but respects himself and asks the question "Does this serve my highest good?" If the answer is 'NO' then **don't do it**. I have written more on this subject later.

Lights On - Lights Off

Imagine that your self-esteem is like tiny lights that you can switch on and off within your body. As you practise / show / demonstrate self -respect or self-love – you switch lights '**on**'. If you deny / abuse your self/ your self respect – you switch lights '**off**'.

By 'deny' I mean – refusing to accept gifts like compliments, treats, and special moments. It also means denying who you are, and what you have to offer to society.

By 'abuse' I mean – over eating, drinking excessive amounts of alcohol, taking unnecessary medication – prescribed or not and allowing your body to be abused – either sexually or physically.

Which of these do you choose to do ?? - switch ON or switch OFF

Try this out – now.

Close your eyes and see how many lights are **on** - right now. If there are not too many on, then you need to switch on some more – **right now** !!

This takes some practise. Imagine yourself switching lights on. Use whatever image that you can see clearly in your mind.

For example, imagine plugging in a set of Christmas lights and watching them all burst into life, all at the same time.

You could imagine a series of light switches on a wall panel. One by one, switch them on.

How does that feel ?

Become aware of how many lights are switched 'ON' and how many lights are switched 'OFF'.

Just by using your imagination you can increase your self-esteem and self-love !!

This may sound like a bold statement, but did you know that your mind cannot tell the difference between 'imagination' and 'reality'??

Your mind cannot tell the difference – there is no line drawn between imagination and reality. You can use this simple fact to your advantage – everyday.

When you continue to imagine lights switching 'ON', in time, you will begin to notice the changes in your attitude to life.

Of course, you can use this technique to 'imagine' and attract lots of other goals into your life.

For example:

You can use this for sports enhancement.

This is how champion sportsmen and women are in a different league from their fellow competitors. Not only do they train very hard, but they also 'train' their mind as well. They use their imagination to 'see' themselves winning, to see themselves running faster, to see themselves jumping higher or further, and so on. They <u>never</u> 'see' themselves fail.

You can use this simple technique to improve your performance throughout your life ??

In an experiment with athletes, scientists 'wired up' each athlete to monitor and record the reaction of each muscle when they ran a race.

They then asked the athlete to sit down and imagine running the same race – they noticed that the athletes used exactly the same muscles – **in their mind**. Their brains reacted *as if* each muscle was actually being used.

Why not imagine yourself being healthy ?

Why not imagine your perfect job ?

Why not imagine being successful ?

If your mind cannot tell the difference between 'imagination' and 'reality', and your mind creates your reality, why not imagine your life the way you would like it to be ??

Whatever man can conceive –

He can achieve !!

My story

How did I get to where I am now ??

When I look back on my life, I often wonder how I survived some of the traumas and difficulties I experienced. These traumas were not just physical traumas but emotional, spiritual and financial. Don't get me wrong, I am not going to tell a hard luck story in order to gain your sympathy. I am like millions of others who have had their ups and downs.

Since 2001, I have studied, attended seminars on personal development, listened to tapes and CDs by eminent entrepreneurs and spiritual masters, I have re-educated myself by training to become a Hypnotherapist, Meridian Therapist and Life Coach.

Throughout this time, I have had the opportunity to look back and re-evaluate my past and replace the negative emotions and pain with 'learning'.

I have realised that every event, every letdown, every disaster has been placed in front of me in order for me to learn and grow from the experience.

I've realised that this is exactly what I am doing on this planet, at this time and in this body – I am

11

learning !! If I choose to ignore this fact, then my life becomes meaningless, uninteresting and unfulfilling.

If there is one thing that I have learnt, it is this - **most of the traumas and disasters were caused by me** !!

Of course, other people and events caused some of these, but I now realise that the quality of my life – right now – comes down to the choices I have made throughout my life.

Some would say that I made some pretty lousy choices. I say that I simply made choices.

Some choices turned out to be 'bad' or 'wrong' with hindsight, but then, when was the last time you <u>deliberately</u> made a 'bad' or 'wrong' choice ? I honestly can't remember my last one.

We all make choices based on the information available to us at the time. It doesn't serve you to punish yourself for the rest of your life, because of a 'bad' choice. This is where guilt comes into its own.

So - Ditch the guilt !!

Making choices is how we develop as people. If every choice were the 'right' one, then you would not learn as much as through making the occasional 'wrong' or 'bad' choice.

Remember, along with making choices comes the matter of 'Responsibility'. Responsibility is the *ability* to *respond* to a given situation – that's all!!

Throughout this book, I hope to raise your awareness to – not only your choices and responsibilities - but to lots more.

The following statement came to me in meditation one day. I struggled with the meaning at first, but then I realised that it was a very profound message for me.

What does it mean to you ??

When you know yourself

you know everything.

Throughout this book take some time out to discover the **'real you'**.

Take some time every day to challenge your beliefs –testing - to the limit - the things in your life that hold you back from achieving what you want in your life.

My Story

The following 8 Kerinsian Keys are not set out in any particular order or preference. That way, you can skip from one Key to another.

Use them to enhance your relationships and your health and your attitude to life.

If you can only pick up one 'gem' that makes a positive change to you, then this little book will be a success and worthwhile. My wish for you is that you will pick up lots of 'gems'.

If you have comments please contact me by email:

bill@billkerins.com

Key 1

Creative Manifestation

Creative Manifestation

Creative Manifestation is the term I use for bringing into your life the material things, people and events that you wish for.

Some have called it – Cosmic Ordering or Creative Visualisation or The Universal Law of Attraction. It doesn't really matter what you call it, so long as you learn the basic strategies and practise them regularly.

So, what does this all mean? Does it mean that you can order up whatever you want and it is delivered to your door?? Well, in a way, yes it does, but it is not as flippant and avaricious as that. It requires thought, focus and patience.

There are so many different teachings on this subject. I am introducing you to the methods that I use and I know work. Over a number of years, I have watched people, material things and events come into my life, and wondered *how* and sometimes more importantly – *why.*

Have you ever wished for something and lo and behold it turns up??

Have you ever wished for something and it doesn't turn up ?? What was the difference ?? You asked

17

for something, so why didn't it turn up ?? I have a couple of ideas about that.

When we 'wish' for something, or for some event to happen, or for some special person to come into our life, we rarely give it a lot of forethought or planning. We tend to blissfully wish for something and not use the techniques of **Creative Manifestation**.

I have listed some of these rules and invite you to use them and notice the benefits. You can adapt them to suit your beliefs and needs.

Be patient and remember:

> **Infinite patience brings immediate results**

> The first rule of Manifestation is: **Use positive language**.

Esther and Jerry Hicks have written a book called *'Ask and it will be given'*. This is a slant on the teachings of the great Master Jesus Christ who used similar words. Basically, he said that whatever we ask for - we can receive.

Messrs Hicks describe human beings being likened to human magnetic fields. We attract into our lives things that we focus on.

I believe this to be true. Strangely enough, I have found this to be relevant when I *don't* want something to happen – and it does happen. Have you ever been carrying a drink across a newly polished floor and not wanting to spill it – and you do !! That was because you were focussing on the word 'spill'.

I'm sure you have plenty of examples of getting what you *don't* want. For some strange reason the universe doesn't hear or deletes the negative words like 'don't'. When you are making your wish list later, make sure you do not include negatives like – "I *don't* want to be poor" – "I *don't* want to be ill". The universe listens and then eliminates the negative word 'don't'. Strange isn't it ??

19

Examples of positive language would be:

"I have a loving and fulfilling personal relationship"

"My life is filled with love and prosperity"

Write down some of your own examples.

"   "

....

"   "

....

"   "

....

"   "

....

"   "

....

"   "

....

"   "

....

"   "

....

> The second rule of Manifestation is: **Use clean language.**

By this I mean, use straightforward, uncomplicated language.

Even in our everyday world, we tend to use mixed up and complicated language. It seems to me that our education systems have ignored the fact that it is imperative that we use clean language.

By clean language I mean:

"I have a prosperous and vibrant business."

"I have a well paid and stimulating job."

"I wish for a happy and healthy relationship."

Don't ask for something and then add in a couple of conditions.

Example: **"I would like to be working in a career that earns me £50,000 a year –** *not one that's too far away."*

"not one without a company car."

Very simply - do not complicate the request.

The third rule of Manifestation is: **Write it down**

Writing down your wish etc. transforms your thought form into a more physical form. It takes the process a step higher and closer to your goal.

- Buy a journal or a notebook.

- Delegate a section to your wishes / needs / intentions.

Then:

- Write today's date at the top of the page.

- Use the first two rules. Write your wishes into your journal.

You can write as many wishes as you can think of at this time. Remember, the universe is abundant, and can provide *all of us* with *all of* our needs. There is no competition – no lack – no need to get there before someone else – no hurry.

If you would like read more on the benefits of writing down your dreams / wishes / requests check out a book called **'Write it Down – Make it Happen'** by **Henriette Anne Klauser**. Published by Simon & Schuster.

In this publication, the author describes in more detail the reasons and benefits on writing down your dreams. She gives examples of how others have achieved seemingly impossible dreams and teaches you how to do it for yourself.

By writing down your wishes and dreams, you are also clarifying exactly what it is you want to manifest.

Very often we ask for things to come into our lives that we <u>think</u> we want, only to find out later that we were greedy or unrealistic.

When you are carrying out this exercise, take your time. Allow time to write things down and then maybe cross things out or re-write them in a different way.

After all, you are creating <u>your life</u>, so take your time and make the most of it.

The fourth rule of Manifestation is: **Use the present tense**

When we make a wish, we tend to ask for something to happen in the future. That sounds reasonable and sensible, but, the universe listens and pays attention to every word. So, if your request is " *I will have more money in my life*" – the universe hears you asking for something that 'will' happen and then delivers it - in the future.

But, of course, the future is always tomorrow or the next day, or next week or next year.

You probably have done this throughout your life and wonder why you have many *'wants'* in your life. Now you know why !!

If your request is " *I am going to be successful*", the universe hears what your are *'going'* to be and delivers that – in the future. Why ? Because you have projected your wish into the future.

So, using the present tense ensures that the universe doesn't get confused about *'when'* you want this wish to manifest.

Examples: "I *am* a successful person - now"
"I *have* a beautiful home to live in - now"
"I *feel* physically fit in every way - now"

24

When you write down **positive** and **clear** statements in the **present tense**, you are well on the way to successful Creative Manifesting.

The fifth rule of Manifestation is: **Visualisation**

If you can close your eyes and imagine something, then you can creatively manifest. Your mind is a wonderful tool that is often – if not always – under-used.

Remember - your mind cannot tell the difference between *imagination* and *reality* ??

This is where illusionists make their living. Your mind can - and often does – fool you into thinking and believing all sorts of things. Our religions utilise this concept – big time. They instil belief systems into our minds, and we subsequently react to those beliefs. *"If you behave like that – you will go to hell"*. Do you remember that one ?? I do, and I remember living a life of fear. And where does fear live ?? – in our mind. I decided to change my mind about those programs and make up my own mind about what was right for me and what was not. And do you know what ?– it has worked.

So, getting back to the power of our minds. It has become clearly evident in recent scientific experiments that we can create emotional and physical changes in our bodies and outside of our bodies by simply 'thinking' positive or negative thoughts.

Dr. David Hamilton in his book **'It's the thought that counts'** has related several experiments to demonstrate this fact. It is worthwhile checking this great book out.

Lynne McTaggart in her book **'The Field'** has conducted research into quantum physics and has concluded that the observer can influence scientific evidence. In other words, the person carrying out the experiment can unconsciously effect the result – <u>through the power of thought !!</u>

It has been scientifically proven that our thoughts effect our immune system. We can actually weaken our immunity to disease by focussing our minds on negative thoughts.

How can you use this powerful tool to create your dreams ??

Here's how. Learn self-hypnosis or how to meditate, whichever you wish to call it at this time. If you know nothing about these two subjects, let me briefly explain.

Both of these phenomena slow down your brainwaves from the Beta state down into the Alpha state. It is not sleep (the Theta state) – but just above the sleep state. When your mind is in this state, you can access your subconscious (or unconscious) mind. It is like opening the door to your subconscious. By accessing your subconscious mind, you can use your imagination to create whatever it is you desire.

You have done this hundreds of thousands of times in the past, without even knowing you were doing it!

By focussing your attention on your wish - you reinforce the creation process. I suggest that you carry out this 'meditation' once and then leave it to the universe to deliver.

In 1989, I read a book called 'The Magus of Strovolus'. He was a very powerful and mystical man, who demonstrated extraordinary healing abilities among other attributes. I decided to look him up, and find out what we were here for, and how we create our lives in a positive and fulfilling way. He lived in a village outside of Nicosia in Cyprus called 'Strovolus'. I was expecting to meet a 'Guru' in long robes and a beard. To my amazement, he was dressed very normally, and lived in an ordinary house in a street in the village. He had been a civil servant when he was a younger man.

He spent several hours teaching me how to manifest, and explaining what was my life's purpose and many more fascinating topics. Regrettably, he died round about 1996.

He taught this process to me. He called it **'Creating Elementals'**. His method was like this:

Visualise your 'elemental' –clearly and accurately – imagine that you have folded it into a ball and then throw it out into space – and then **let it be**.

Don't go back and change it everyday. Don't worry about it not arriving.
Just **let it be**.

If you would like to learn more about this extraordinary man, I suggest you read:

'The Magus of Strovolus' by **Kyriacos C. Markides.**

As you can see, there are many ways to visualise. Try each one and find the one that works best for you.

> The sixth rule of Manifestation is: **Acceptance**

Acceptance for some, could be the difficult bit !

In Tao Buddhism, they say:

What is – is

Basically, this means that there are some things that are the way they are, and cannot be changed.

If today is Wednesday, there is no point in trying to change it to Tuesday or Thursday. It is the way it is.

If you have lost something in life – a loved one, a job opportunity or maybe property – you cannot change that fact. But, we, as human beings, spend and waste a lot of our energy on looking back at what 'might have been', or how we might be able to change it. The only thing that we <u>can</u> change is:

How we feel about it !!

Acceptance is easy when things are going your way. When your wishes or dreams are coming through, it is easy to accept. But when it seems that your wishes are not arriving on time and in the right way, it becomes a little more difficult.

Acceptance is allowing the universe to deliver in accordance with its *Divine Plan* and for the highest good of all.

What does this mean ?? I hear you ask.

When you create something in your life, you then let it be – and then get ready to *accept* the 'gift' or 'wish'.   But, you are also asked to be willing to *accept* the fact that it might not happen.

It is a difficult concept to get your head around, but, when you do, life becomes easier and seems to flow better.

Can you imagine how much energy you expend on getting frustrated and angry at people, things and events that we have absolutely no control over ??

I believe that the universe in evolving perfectly.   I also believe that there must be some force that controls the movement of planets etc. In order for this to continue throughout millions of years, without things bumping into each other, there must be order. I <u>know</u> that this order is working perfectly.

So, to keep things in order, the universe must 'have it's way', hence it delivers what is in accordance with the Divine Plan – **and nothing else !!**

It is all about total trust in the universe (or God, or whatever you want to call it), and knowing that everything that happens, happens for a good reason, which is for the highest good of all the universe.

It has taken me a great number of years to learn and accept this simple concept, simply because I wanted to be in control of every thing in my life. That was my ego. My lesson has been to **'let go and let God'**. Let it be yours.

Sometimes, we *think* we need something and we wish and pray for it, only to find that, in the end, it wasn't really what we really wanted.

Remember:

We don't always get what we want –

but, we always get what we need !!

32

> The seventh rule of Manifestation is: **Gratitude**

The final and probably the most important rule is –
Gratitude.

Always remember to be grateful for everything you receive in your life. The good, the bad, and even, the ugly.

Everything comes into your life with a purpose. Your task is to learn the lesson behind every event – every encounter – every relationship – every illness.

We come into this life to learn, and these events, things and people are messengers delivering the lesson. It makes sense of some of the more bizarre, sinister and sometimes crazy events that we encounter throughout our lives. One of the most profound lessons is to say 'Thank You' for the lesson – including the crazy lesson.

> ### So - Don't shoot the messenger !!

Every evening, just as you turn your light out to go to sleep, say a prayer of thanks. If you are a spiritual person, you will know to whom you are saying 'thank you'. If you are not, say 'thank you' anyway!

33

When you say 'thank you' – just quietly listen for a reply. You may be in for a surprise.

If you listen carefully, you may hear a little voice inside your head saying something like – 'You are welcome'.

It never ceases to amaze me when I do this little exercise. I always have a sense of peace and calm. It also helps me to sleep. It helps me feel that I am not alone. It gives me:

The serenity to accept the things I cannot change,

The courage to change the things I can

and

The wisdom to know the difference

I have written more on this subject in Key 8.

Key 2

Relationships

Relationships

Unless you live on a desert island, you are going to be affected by relationships. Relationships are what we are all about.

Did you know that if you were dropped onto a desert island at the age of twelve and never met another soul for forty years, you would not develop emotionally much further than a twelve year old. We need relationships in order to grow.

Now, I'm not just talking about one to one relationships e.g. boyfriend / girlfriend; husband / wife relationships, I'm talking about everyone you come into contact with throughout your life. Your next door neighbour – and everyone else on your street – your boss, work colleagues, friends, social contacts, business contacts, your family, casual acquaintances etc. We were born to form relationships.

I would like you to use your imagination. Imagine that you had a bubble around you, spreading out in every direction. This bubble is about six feet in diameter. This imaginary bubble could be described similar to your aura. As you are the one to have shaped and grown this bubble, you are also responsible for the colour of it.

37

Yes, the colour, because I want you to imagine that the colour represents the emotional place you are in right now. It doesn't matter what colour it is, because everyone has produced his or her own colour.

So bright colours don't mean that you are better or brighter than someone with a dark colour. It simply means that your colour is distinct to you.

For example, imagine if you are red and the other person (your partner / friend / boss) is blue.

As you grow emotionally, your colour constantly changes.

You cannot help or control this process. When we form any relationship, we <u>partially</u> overlap our colour with the other person. I call this overlap our *relationship*. If you can imagine red overlapping with blue it creates a new colour.

This colour is unique to <u>your</u> relationship with that person <u>at that time</u>. As you grow through time (and you cannot stop this process) your colour and your partner's colour changes. When you originally formed the relationship, both of you, subconsciously or emotionally, resonated with that relationship colour, otherwise you wouldn't have formed the relationship in the first place.

As you both grow, become aware that the 'colour' of your relationship also changes. This is how people become closer or grow apart. The colour of your relationship has changed, and you may or may not like the new one. If you grow apart, you may search for the old one. But you will never find the old one, because it is in the past, and a different you.

What you will find – if you choose to look – is a new colour. But, you may not like this colour and then decide to end the relationship, if it does not resonate with you. Let this decision be **your** decision alone – one that is for **your** highest good.

In some ways, it is similar to eating food that you used to like, and don't like now - but continue to eat it anyway. Why would you do that ?? It doesn't make sense does it ?

Remember – people change – **you** are constantly changing - and my message here is this:

- Be aware of the changes going on in your life.

- Take charge of how you are going to cope with these changes.

- Act responsibly and positively to each change.

Relationships have to be constantly worked on. So many people move into a relationship and then stop working on it.

Become aware of the subtle changes that are going on in your relationship, and work towards making these changes enhance your relationship – not diminish it.

It is worth it in the end. **You** are worth it in the end.

Self love

Which brings me to the relationship you are having with yourself. You may have heard the expression:

> *'You come in alone and you leave alone.'*

However, in between being born and dying, there is a space in time called 'your life' in which you have a responsibility to 'YOU'.

To me, the most important relationship you are likely to have, is the relationship you have with yourself.

By this, I mean, your welfare, your health, your personal development, your spiritual development and your happiness. In order for you to have a happy and successful relationship with yourself you must learn to **love yourself**.

I don't mean a 'selfish' love but a 'self-full' love. There is a difference. Let me explain each.

A *selfish love* is an 'I'm alright Jack' type of relationship. It is a relationship that offers nothing to anyone else but you. In fact, it sometimes takes away from those around you as well. It is an EGO driven relationship, which results in <u>un</u>happiness and heartache. It is an insecurity, which encourages you to look outside of yourself for things, substances or experiences to fulfil the need for self-love.

A *self-full love* is different inasmuch as it is about fulfilling your needs, without causing distress to yourself or those around you. It is about recognising your worth and deservability, and fully accepting *you* as you are - right now !!

It is not about thinking that you are the greatest gift to mankind and that you know everything. One of the greatest exponents of self-love of our modern age is **Louise L. Hay**. Her books, tapes and lectures explain in detail how she, and you can change your way of thinking about yourself.

Self-love is the purest form of love, and should not be seen as an ego exercise, but more of a personal development exercise.

41

How do I learn to love myself more ?

Here are some exercises, which will start you on the road to self-love.

- Everyday – treat yourself to a gift. This could be as simple as a walk in the woods or by the sea. It could be buying yourself an ice cream and really relishing it, or taking an hour to watch afternoon television. It could be calling someone you really enjoy talking to, and spending an hour chatting. Treat yourself with awareness.

- Notice every time you have a negative thought about yourself e.g. "oh! I forgot to call .... , I'm really stupid." Consciously change this thought and this kind of self speak. Remember – every thought and every word creates your reality.

- Whenever you are asked to do something that you really don't want to do, think about how you will *feel* if you do it. If it makes you feel bad or uneasy, then ___**don't do it**___ . If you do, you are only lowering your self worth / self-esteem. Switching lights off.

- Be grateful for the little things in your daily life. Say 'Thank you' more often. When you express gratitude to another person you blend your energy field with theirs. When you do this often

42

enough, you become more empathic, more loving towards others and of course, more self-aware.

We judge the quality of our lives by the way people and relationships effect us.

Life is like friendship – it is not a big thing, it is a million little things.

Become aware of the little 'gems' in your life and show appreciation for all of them.

For example:

- a hug from your child / lover.

- a complement from a friend / lover about your looks.

- an unexpected gift from a friend – or a casual acquaintance.

- a visit by a friend, just when you need a shoulder to cry on.

Remember:

Always be grateful !

and show your appreciation

43

This simple act can enhance your relationships in so many ways.

Communication

My experience of relationships has shown me time and time again that one of the major factors in relationship breakdown is a lack of communication.

My wife doesn't understand me !!

How many times have you heard that one??

Isn't it strange that we can talk to complete strangers about our issues and problems, and not be able to talk to our spouse or partner ?

When you first met, you probably talked for hours, but now that the relationship has 'matured', you don't seem to have the time or inclination to discuss your relationship.

A very effective and simple technique you can use is what I call 'ten minutes each way'.

This is what you do.

Ten minutes each way

- Set aside a time (30 minutes) to sit down and discuss what is going on for both of you.

- Make sure that you will not be disturbed by children, friends etc.

- Switch off the phone – and mobile phone if you have one.

- Decide on who goes first – person 'A'

- As person 'A' you are allowed to talk uninterrupted for ten minutes, with no corrections or facial expressions of disagreement from person 'B'.

- You can talk about your feelings, how your relationship is going for you. Talk about the changes that are happening and how you are feeling about them. You can talk about any subject you wish – keeping in mind that you are focussing on your relationship.

- Even if you have nothing to say, you are still entitled to your ten minutes.

- After ten minutes, change over.

- Person 'B' is <u>not</u> allowed to take time to 'correct' the comments made by person 'A'.

- Person 'B' now has ten minutes to relate thoughts and feelings etc.

- If you like, you can then spend the remaining ten minutes <u>agreeing</u> on how you can both contribute to improving your relationship.

The benefits of this exercise are:

- You learn to listen and to hear your partner.

- You learn to be honest with your partner.

- You become more aware of your partner's needs.

- You become more aware of <u>your</u> needs.

- Both of you are taking control of the direction your relationship is moving towards.

I suggest that you carry out this technique once every two or three weeks – or more often if you find it is working really well.

Being able to express yourself is one of life's saving graces. It is well documented that those who harbour their thoughts and never express them suffer more from mental and physical illness. It is like having the needle stuck in the groove. The thoughts go round and round in your head, resulting in stress, anger and frustration.

When you speak to each other – speak your truth. Isn't it better to hear your truth and your partner's truth ?

That way, you can make clearer and more defined decisions about your future. Otherwise, you can spend a great deal of (wasted) time fooling yourself and those around you.

And the truth shall set you free.

Key 3

Spiritual Connection

Spiritual Connection

Spiritual connection is not an easy subject to discuss, because each one of us has different ways to connect with spirit.

Just for a moment, imagine that you have a spirit guide / a guardian angel by your side at all times.

Then imagine that this guide has access to lots more information and wisdom that you would consciously be aware of.

What would you do when you were in times of doubt, fear or confusion ? You would be fool to ignore the fact that this divine being is close to you and willing, in fact, dying to help ?

Unfortunately, most people do ignore this fact and struggle on 'alone'. Of course, feeling alone is probably one of the worst conditions to experience.

Throughout millennia, mankind has searched the heavens for spiritual guidance. They have built towers to heaven in order to access this great power – to no avail. The reason for the failure was that they were looking outside of themselves for spirit and forgot or ignored the simple truth, which is – *spirit is within*. They were simply looking in the wrong place. We have within our being a spirit of enormous proportions. This spirit is ready to assist us

51

with every conflict, illness and problem in our lives – if we ask. This, I believe, is what leaves our bodies when we die. It is the very essence or energy of our human life. Without it – we are dead.

Did you ever 'hear' a voice or pick up a thought that appeared to come out of nowhere ? Did you ever suddenly slow down your car and then discover that you avoided a potential accident ahead ? What or who was that ?

It was your guide(s) warning you. Sometimes it comes as a feeling. Sometimes it comes as a voice.

Maybe I'm fooling myself here, but for me, it works. I am happy with that. But do you know something else ? If I ignore these 'supernatural' warnings, I feel stupid and angry with myself, which in turn contributes to my self-esteem being lowered. I call this low self-esteem a 'disconnection from spirit'.

How do I correct this ?

I meditate !! I ask for help and guidance from my spirit guides. I remember my past experiences with spirit. I thank spirit for helping in the past and ask for help in the future.

To me, meditation is similar to building muscles. You do a little today and some more tomorrow. In time, like bodybuilding, you will begin to notice subtle changes to all areas of your life.

If you don't know how to meditate and would like to find out more about meditation – go to Key 6

For me, spiritual connection is not a 'Sunday thing'. It is not something I call on whenever my life is in a mess. It is an everyday thing.

This is what I call - **"Walking my talk"**

Now, I would be lying if I were to claim that this is a constant for me, but it is something that I am constantly working on. It is a **'work in progress'**.

I often forget that I am not alone. I often forget to ask for help in times of trouble. I need to be reminded, but, when I do reconnect with spirit, I find that things turn around very quickly. I find that my thoughts are clearer and more positive. Of course, when that happens, my mood is lighter, my life is more abundant and regular.

When I connect with spirit, I am a happier person. When I am happier, my relationships are happier – and I attract all sorts of good things into my life.

Love is life's most sought after gift.
The second most sought after gift is **'inner peace'**.

Both of these are available when you connect with spirit – and <u>never</u> available when you are disconnected. Have you ever met an angry, violent and bitter **spiritual** person ??

It is no coincidence that truly spiritual leaders are those who lead by example and are constantly 'in peace' and 'in love'. Examples of these great people are:

The Dalai Lama,

Sai Baba,

Ghandi,

Mother Therese,

Jesus Christ,

The Buddha.

YOU

Maybe you could add your name to the list !!

Close your eyes for a moment and imagine your name alongside these great people. How good would that feel ??

Key 4

Health & Wellbeing

Health & Wellbeing

Most of us go through our daily lives without giving much thought to our health and wellbeing. We take for granted the fact that we eat, drink and breathe. We remain unconscious to the fact that our cellular structure, our immune system, our nervous systems are working their backsides off, in order to keep us going on a day to day basis.

And, of course, this is to be expected. We cannot be expected to focus our attention on these systems working correctly minute by minute throughout the day. We would probably go mad, and get nothing else done.

But I am suggesting that you spend some time paying attention to these functions in order to correct any misuse or abuse of your body – your health and wellbeing.

Simple things to consider.

- How much sleep do you take – is it enough or too much ?

- How much exercise do you take ?

- How much water do you drink each day ?

- How much recreation do you take ? How much playtime do you include in your everyday life ??

- Food – are you aware of the quality and quantity of your food intake ?? In a busy world, we often eat because it is time to eat or we eat because we are hungry.

- How much alcohol (and other substances) do you consume that may damage your body ??

But health and wellbeing is not just about food and exercise. It is also about your lifestyle. Take, for example, the quality of your life.

Most of us work hard and some of us play hard. The effect of hard living takes its toll over a period of time.

Have you ever considered the effect of how stress effects our daily wellbeing ?? I am talking about negative stress. We hear about the need for some stress in our lives, in order to produce better results from our work and play. This is called positive stress and, of course, it works well when it comes to work related issues and sports performance.

However, I'm talking about negative stress.

Negative stress is the feeling you get when things seem to be getting out of control.

The metaphor I use for this is:

Imagine you have a car on the crest of a hill and you are trying to stop it from rolling down the hill. When the car is stopped, it is easy to hold it in place, by leaning on the bonnet for example. Imagine if someone – or something started to push the back of the car. Obviously, it would take a little more effort to prevent it rolling down the hill. But, if you are strong enough, you will resist. If more and more pressure is applied, you will soon be unable to resist the movement and you would lose control.

This is exactly what stress is like. At first, we hardly notice the stress. Then, as we feel more pressure, we find it harder to resist and become weaker. In time, we find that we are unable to hold it back and we move into serious stress.

The car starts rolling down the hill and we are out of control.

What can you do about this runaway car ??

• You may need to recruit help.

• You may need to apply the brakes

• Sometimes, you may need to get out of the way before you are run over

• Maybe, you need to say 'NO'.

59

Stress management is becoming a major part of our modern lifestyle. But, instead of managing stress we could be looking at ways to eliminate negative stress from our lives in the first instance.

By this, I mean, instead of waiting for stress to appear in our lives, and then 'dealing' with it, we could be looking at ways to avoid it in the first place.

Prevention is better than cure

This is an old but true saying.

How do you prevent stress ??

Here are some methods for you to ponder.

- Learn to recognise the signs of stress:

  Constant irritability
  Difficulty in sleeping
  Preoccupation – mind wandering
  Unable to focus – lack of concentration
  Excessive drinking of alcohol – more than usual
  Physical pain – in your shoulders, back, migraine headaches,
  Crying for no apparent reason
  Lack of libido.

- Learn to say 'NO' to extra demands. This is not always easy, but remember – you will be unable to do *anything*, never mind *extra* work, if you have a breakdown.

- Become more aware of balancing leisure with demanding work - have fun. Remember, this is the only body you are likely to have in this lifetime. Look after it as well as you can.

  In the end, you will be pleased that you did, and you will be 'honouring' your body, which, in turn, honours **YOU** as a physical and spiritual being.

- Exercise – a small amount of exercise releases seratonin in the brain, which will help you to feel good. Exercise will also help to release tension that may be building up in your system.

Become pro-active when dealing with stress and not re-active to the symptoms.

The Kerinsian Law of Cause and Effect

Be the **cause** of your own life

not the **effect** of someone else's life.

Water

By now, most of us know that our body is made up of 72% water – and our brain is made up of 92% water. So as you can see, water is vital to our wellbeing. There are all sorts of theories about the amount of water that we 'should' drink every day. Some say 2 litres a day, others say less than that.

I'm not a medically trained person, and would not legislate as to how much you 'should' drink, but, I would suggest that you become more of a water drinker than a coke, coffee or alcohol drinker.

Dehydration, and not muscle or mental fatigue causes most tiredness. We often feel tired when we haven't actually being doing anything physical to make us tired. It is most likely to be dehydration.

The message here is:

Drink more water !!

To find out about the amazing changes you can make to water, read **'Messages from Water'** by Masaru Emoto. He claims that you can change the molecular structure of water simply by focussing positive thoughts towards it. I believe he is right.

Water helps to:

- flush out the toxins in your body.

- lubricate your joints.

- reduce inflammation in the body – indigestion, arthritis, stomach ulcers and more.

- carry electrical impulses throughout your brain.

Water is the most common element on the planet and the most useful one.

Key 5

Total Awareness

Total Awareness

Did you ever break a habit or routine? Do you remember having a habit like – biting your nails? How did you change this?

Normally, you break a habit by becoming acutely aware that you are doing it in the first place, or someone brings it to your attention.

You notice that you are biting your nails and then you take your fingers out of your mouth and stop.

A few minutes later you notice that you are doing it again, and again, you stop.

If you keep doing this exercise, you will eventually stop biting your nails.

What you are actually doing is this. You are retraining your brain **not** to bite your nails. When you form habits, learn new skills, or do any routine exercise your brain 'forms a neuropath' from one area of your brain to another. The more you do something, the more of a 'habit' it becomes. This is how factory workers can carry out repetitive tasks all day, without having to consciously think about it. This is how you drive your car, and carry on a conversation at the same time. Your brain is entrained to drive the car. You are not consciously 'aware' that you are changing gears, indicating, braking etc.

When you follow a habit or a routine, it is like dropping a needle onto the record and playing the tune. The needle follows the track and the same tune is played over and over again.

Take a routine exercise that you do every day, like the school run. Most parents do it because they **have to!** You bundle your precious cargo into the car, sit in traffic, and become more and more irritable because of slow traffic and noisy kids. Finally, you get there, drop them off and trek home again or on to work or to the shops.

Did you ever become aware of all of the negative feelings that are involved here? Irritability, impatience, disrespect, non- achievement, anger - with yourself and your little darlings. None of these feelings are contributing to your happiness or sense of wellbeing.

This is just one item in your busy day.

There are many more routines that we carry out day after day, without becoming aware that we can actually do something about changing them. We become irritable with our partners and children because we are irritable with ourselves, but we don't acknowledge it to ourselves.

You can change this by becoming more aware. How many more things that irritate you can you think of now? Write them down - now.

1. ....

2. ....

3. ....

4. ....

5. ....

6. ....

7. ....

8. ....

9. ....

10. ....

*"How can I change these feelings if I **have to** continue to take the kids to school.?"*

Become aware !!

You can change these feelings by paying attention to those feelings while you are carrying out your task. Notice your thoughts while driving through the slow traffic and then change your thoughts to positive, fun, motivating thoughts.

Look for the good things in this exercise.

• Think of how lucky you are to have **healthy noisy kids** and smile to yourself.

• Be thankful for the fact that you **have** a car to drive them to school.

• Be thankful for the fact that you are **healthy and skilled** enough to be able to do this task every day, and so on.

Look for the learning opportunities !

• You have time to spend with your children.

• You have time to reflect on the good parts of your life and to plan your day in a positive way.

I don't always enjoy driving, so, I use the time constructively. Instead of taking a long journey in a bad mood, I use the time to listen to music or a recording by Dr. Wayne Dyer or Anthony Robbins or some other inspirational speaker.

"How do I become more aware?"

At times, this lack of awareness can be so frustrating, which leads to more and more mis-judgements and mistakes. This can be costly – not only to our wallets, but also to our time and energy.

There are several exercises that are simple, short and effective. It is not only those people who appear to be very busy that are unaware. Unawareness or lack of awareness is also a trait of the unemployed, under employed and non-employed.

Some people who have little to do can drift into a world of unawareness, simply because they don't want to spend time getting in touch with their feelings. Maybe, this is because they are afraid that they might end up feeling depressed or not good enough.

But it is not about getting depressed and feeling miserable, actually it's the opposite. It is about recognising your feelings and then doing something about them. It is my opinion that *my life* is all about how *I feel*.

If I feel good - then life is good

If I feel bad - then life is bad.

71

Scientists now know that we influence our environment, our health and well being through our thought patterns. We have all had an experience of hearing a noise at night and frightening ourselves rigid just by *thinking* about the noise and what might be causing it.

We actually can affect our body by thinking either negative thoughts or positive thoughts. Often, we are totally unaware of what we are thinking, and how we are thinking. What paths do your thoughts take ?

Here is an example:

You go shopping to the supermarket and then realise that you left the shopping list at home. What do you say to yourself ? Do you:

- Chastise yourself for being forgetful – "Oh I'm so stupid"

- Rant and rave in your mind, reminding yourself of how dumb you are and that you 'always' forget something

Or do you:

- Instantly forgive yourself and smile about it ?

- Challenge yourself as to how many items from the list you can remember.

I would suggest practising the second list of things to do. This, quite simply, is turning a negative thought into a positive thought. This method of deliberately changing your perception of a situation from negative to positive is very powerful and within your control.

It takes practise, but in time you will notice subtle changes in your mood and general attitude to life – **your** life !!

In order to improve and prove your level of awareness, here are some exercises.

Exercise 1.

You will need a friend to help you with this exercise.

Ask your friend to look around the room you are in, and then close his / her eyes.

Read out these questions and pause between them.

• How many chairs are there in the room?

• What is the colour or pattern of the carpet or floor covering?

• Are there curtains ? If so, what do they look like?

How did your friend do??

Very often, we miss a lot of information about our surroundings, simply by not paying any attention to them ? It's not a requirement that we know every detail of every room in our house, but how aware are you of your surroundings in general?

Exercise 2.

You can do this exercise alone. If you like, you can ask one question at a time and stop to write down your answer.

With your eyes closed, ask yourself these questions:

- How am I feeling right now? Contented? Happy? Angry? Peaceful?

- How do I feel my life is going right now?

- What am I feeling about the future? Excited? Fearful?

- One thing that I would change right now in order to improve my life would be ……

What answers did you get?

Did you find the answers interesting ?

Were they different when you took time to think (become aware) of the questions ?

When you become aware of these answers, you can start to do something about them.

When you become aware that you are angry, then you can do something about the anger. There are so many ways to dissipate anger – go for a run, punch a pillow – (not another living being), scream out loud, dance around the room to heavy rock music, talk to someone.

The main lesson here is:

Identify (become aware of) your feelings – then do something about them.

If you find that your life is not so good at the moment, then take steps to correct this. Very often, we are feeling low are and unaware of it.

If you are fearful of the future, ask yourself "what is the absolute worst thing that could happen".

When you answer this, you can start to take steps to prevent that happening. If you can imagine or 'see' the worst case scenario, then anything less than that is good. Anything less is better than the worst case scenario. That alone is helping you to tackle the issue and improve on it.

In other words - take control of your life. After all, it is your life. Why leave it to someone else to take over control your life. It might only irritate someone else, and anyway – it is not their life – it's **yours !!**

Exercise 3.

Take a walk – pay attention and watch out for:

Smells - flowers, cooking smells, perfume in the air.

Cloud formations.

The colours of the trees , look at seasonal changes .

Peoples' faces – are they smiling, contented? What might they be thinking ?

Sounds – birds, children laughing and playing.

Feel – the breeze on your face, the heat of the sun.

When you get home, notice how much different your walk felt.   You may notice that you enjoyed the walk much more, simply because you were more aware of your surroundings.

If you apply these techniques to your life - everyday - you will notice a dramatic change to the way you see life.

Become aware of the good things in your life and refuse to focus on the negative things – the things that can drain your energy.

The purpose of these exercises is to highlight how much we miss when we are unaware. When you think about it, your life is happening **NOW**.

What happens at this moment is all that we have any level of control over. When we unaware, we tend to miss what is going on at this moment, and miss the pleasure and learning from every experience.

Have you ever known or heard of a person who has been given terminal news? e.g. "you have three months to live".

Very often these people become extremely 'aware'. They set out to enjoy every waking moment of their final days. They are aware of the bad feelings between themselves and old friends or family and make every effort to reconcile and make up. They want do the things that they haven't done, see places they haven't seen and many more *vital* experiences.

Why is that ?? Why do we wait until we are in a position like that in order to start enjoying our lives? Why not make it your policy to 'do it now', because

NOW is all the time there is !!

Become more aware!!

There is a story told of a lady whose husband asked her what she would do if she were given three months to live.

She said " Oh, I would sell the house and travel around the world. I would visit exotic places and have a ball of a time. I would shop till I dropped".

The husband smiled and said "yes, if that happened, we <u>could</u> do that."

The lady replied " who said anything about **'we'.**"

Key 6

Meditation

Meditation

Throughout millennia, man has struggled with the idea of meditation. Statements like –

"Meditation is only for those who have the time and discipline to do it."

"Meditation is very difficult, you have to be a special kind of person to do it properly."

To me, the results of meditation create the above. By this I mean, when you learn to meditate, it creates time and discipline. It changes you into a special person – and more, much more.

Meditation is not a matter of sitting cross-legged on top of a hill and chanting mantras with your eyes closed. Mind you, you can choose to do that if you like, but it not actually necessary.

Q. Can anyone meditate ?
A. Yes ! anyone can meditate.

In fact, in lots of ways, we often spend some time during each day in a form of meditation. This is when we find ourselves gazing out the window daydreaming. Our attention or focus is taken to another place or dimension. On one level, we are aware of our immediate surroundings, but on another level, we are miles away.

Technically, our brain is in the 'Alpha' state when we meditate. This is the state just above sleep and below full waking state.

When you practise regular meditation, the benefits are enormous. For example:

- Your blood pressure becomes more regular.

- Every organ in your body relaxes and rejuvenates.

- Your mind calms down, reducing, even eliminating stress.

- You contact another part of yourself – your spiritual connection.

- You rest the muscles in your body – including your face, which in time will help you to look younger and more vibrant but not guaranteed to make you even more beautiful – sorry !

- Your mind becomes clearer, enabling you to make better decisions.

- A ten minute meditation is as beneficial as an hour's sleep.

- You access your healing place or centre – which accelerates the healing process on all forms of physical, mental and emotional levels.

I use meditation to ask for help from my guides. I take the time to 'speak' to them and await the answers. Sometimes the answers come in immediately, and other times I have to be patient. But I find that through practising meditation regularly, my level of patience has risen as well.

Meditation sounds like it is the elixir of life, and in lots of ways it is !! The simple fact that meditation has been practised in every culture and religion throughout the world, for thousands of years is testimony to its powerful effect.

So, "How do I learn to meditate" I hear you ask.

To learn basic meditation techniques you will need the following:

- A comfortable chair.

- A suitable (beginners) meditation CD or tape.

- A CD player with or without headphones.

- A quiet space – with no disturbing elements like kids, television etc.

- Time – whatever amount of time you want to start with. Initially, five to ten minutes is ample.

- Patience – sometimes, it takes several attempts at first to really begin to feel the benefits of meditation. Be patient with yourself and don't expect huge results immediately.

From here, the course is simple. Find the time and space, switch on your CD, sit comfortably and listen.

Don't try to meditate just by closing your eyes and 'blanking' your mind. Because your mind is constantly active, it is going to be very difficult for it to 'shut down', just because you decide to do it.

Once you have mastered the 'art' of light meditation, you can move into higher and higher levels of meditation.

You can also use meditations to resolve issues that are going on in your life. If you are confused about a situation that requires a decision, then meditate on it.

Basically, you are allowing your higher consciousness to come into play. This is like accessing a database of information that contains all of the answers to all of your issues or problems.

At first, when I started to meditate on a regular basis – four to five times a week – I found it difficult to focus and be patient, but, with a little effort, I began to feel calmer, more composed, I was sleeping better, I was thinking clearer.

That was six years ago, and recently, I heard a report that doctors have 'discovered' that meditation is actually very beneficial to our health and general well being. Isn't that amazing ! Our medical doctors have finally discovered something that has been common knowledge among the sages for centuries.

And now for my advertising break.

I have produced a CD that will teach you to meditate called *'Learn to Meditate'*.

If you would like to order one, please go to www.billkerins.com/products and I would be delighted to send one on to you.

Key 7

Physiology

Physiology

Physiology has been defined as " the biological study of the functions of living organisms and their parts".

Basically, it means our physical body effects the functioning of our mental and emotional state – and vice versa.

Your mind will always follow your body.

Your body will always follow your mind.

These statements may seem a little silly but, when you realise that the *condition* of your physical life is governed by the *condition* of your mind.

When you are in a negative state of mind, you may feel sluggish – unable or unwilling to get up and motivate yourself into action. If, someone or something helps to change your mind you can suddenly feel motivated and more alive.

Key 7 - Physiology

What has happened here ??

Because you have 'changed your mind', your body has more energy. You see, the energy was there all the time. You just needed to access it – and you did that through the power of your mind.

I know that you already knew that !! But , I just wanted to remind you that you have within you all of the resources you need in order to have a fulfilling and happy life.

Here are some exercises for times when you feel low.

- Stand in front of a mirror and make silly, funny faces at yourself.

- Notice how the feeling changes from low to higher. This is because when you are smiling, your brain is producing endorphins which help to pick you up and help you to feel better.

- Play some dancing music – loud !! - and start dancing.

- Notice again how the feeling changes. This is because you are energising your Lymphatic system, again producing more endorphins and moving energy around your body. By energising your Lymphatic system, you are helping to clear your body of unwanted toxins.

- If you are sitting slouched in a chair – stand up and exercise – swing your arms, jump up and down. Do anything that will change your physical state. Go for a jog or walk the dog – nice and briskly. When you change your physical state, you change the mental and emotional state as well.

These exercises help change your state of mind by doing something physical. But, remember, you had to change your mind first, in order to get up and move or dance.

What I am saying is this:

When your feeling down or low, <u>do something</u> to take you out of that place.

When your body is feeling low, motivate your mind by focussing on happier times, beautiful people, beautiful places, and happy holidays. Read funny stories, or watch a comedy film on DVD or on the television.

This takes effort, but the benefits are enormous.

- It doesn't cost anything.

- It can be done any time.

- You are taking back control of your mind and body.

- With practise, you can teach this technique to others – **become the living proof that it works !**

The truth is this – no one can 'make ' you feel better. Friends, family and therapists can help, but they cannot change your state of mind. Only you can do that.

Albert Einstein once said:

> # "Nothing happens until something moves."

In order for you to change your life in any way – you must move something.

When you fully understand this simple technique, you can move mountains – easily.

Breathing

Whenever I ask my clients to take a deep breath and fill their lungs with air, they will:

- Raise their shoulders.

- Suck air into their upper chest.

- Pull in their stomach.

When they breathe out they reverse the procedure. This is what is sometimes called **'Reverse Breathing'.**

This is not a 'wrong' way to breathe, but it is not deep breathing. It is useful to do this type of breathing occasionally.

Normal Breathing (also called 'Deep Breathing') is when you breathe in, your abdomen expands, and when you breathe out, it contracts. In relation to Qigong, this type of breathing connects you to your 'Dantien' or centre. This is the area just below your navel.

The Dantien stores our 'Qi' or energy to balance the body.

When you breathe in and expand your abdomen, you push down on your diaphragm, which in turn, pulls more air down to the bottom of your lungs.

Your lungs are pear shaped – narrower at the top than the bottom. By drawing more air to the bottom of your lungs, you are supplying your whole body with more oxygen. As a bonus, when you push down on your diaphragm, you compress the organs in your lower chest and abdomen– spleen, liver, gallbladder and pancreas. This slight compression helps to stimulate these organs and helps them to operate more effectively.

Natural Breathing is breathing without being conscious of where the air is going. It is what we do every day. Use this type of breathing when you meditate.

I mention these types of breathing so that you become aware of your own breathing patterns.

This brings me to posture.

Posture

How you stand or sit determines your wellbeing. If you stand with your shoulders sloped and your head hanging down, your breathing becomes shallow. This reduces the oxygen going to your brain. This results in:

- Tiredness.

- Depression

- Lack of concentration.

- Lack of motivation.

- Slow movement

- And many more debilitating symptoms.

Simply by reversing this stance, you increase the oxygen to your brain and reverse the symptoms.

What would you want people to think and react to when they meet you on the street or in a business or social meeting ??

Take some time to imagine how people would react when they meet you for the first time. You would like to make an impression, and remember – first impressions last. In other words, people make up their minds about the kind of person you are within the first ten to fifteen seconds of meeting you. If that is the 'wrong' impression and you may spend a long time changing that impression.

Behave in the way that you would like to impress people. You will also impress yourself – believe me.

Walking

When you are walking, become aware of your pace, posture and attitude. If you are slouching and dragging your feet, pull yourself up and change to a more positive attitude. This increases the oxygen and will help you to feel better. It may even get you there faster as well !!

Touch

Many research experiments on touch – and the lack of touch - have been carried out with animals and people. Scientists have discovered that baby chimps become more aggressive and inhibited if they are reared in an environment of isolation and without being touched – especially by their mother and siblings.

As chimpanzees are our closest relatives, it is not surprising that this phenomenon also effects humans.

In the past, I have used the art of touch to move a group of people from one room to another. Simply by touching people's elbows, they move much more easily than just by asking them to move.

In an experiment in the USA, researchers set up a TV camera opposite a telephone booth and watched people's reactions. In the first instance, they placed some small change into the coin retriever in the booth. Whenever a person used the phone and checked the receiver, they found the loose change and pocketed it. The researcher then approached the person and said that they had just been using the phone and forgot to take their change.

In 93% of the cases, the person denied taking the change.

They then changed the situation by approaching the person <u>and touching their arm</u>, and asking the same question, the response changed from 93% to 47%.

The only difference was <u>touching their arm</u>. People respond to touch without consciously realising it.

This is why we respond positively to hugs, handshakes and physical closeness. It has something to do with responding to an energy exchange. Children and old folk that live in uncaring homes tend to be unwell in a general sense of the word. They seem to be missing something in their lives – and they are. They are missing the touch of another human being. They can sometimes replace human touch with animal touch, but it's not the same.

Perhaps you would consider visiting one of these homes near to you, and offering your kindness and love to someone whom is desperately in need of a hug.

In our modern world of invasiveness and litigation, it is a shame that we sometimes feel awkward when we reach out to another in a caring way.

Of course, we have to respect the other person's space, but with their permission, they - and you – can benefit enormously from the simple act of hugging.

Learn to use the power of touch in your every day encounters and watch for the response. I think that you will be pleasantly surprised.

Key 8

Attitude of Gratitude

Attitude of Gratitude

As I have mentioned in the chapter on manifestation, an attitude of gratitude is the ability and awareness to be thankful for everything - and I mean everything. In our busy world and lives, we often don't take the opportunity to say 'thank you' for a long list of items in our lives.

For example:

- Our health.

- Our friends.

- Our prosperity.

- Our relationships – personal and business.

- The changes of seasons.

- The beauty of a flower.

- The beauty of a sunset.

- The warmth of the sun.

- The food we eat.

- Our animal friends – pets, wildlife etc.

And so on infinitum.

Whenever I make an appointment with a new client, I give thanks. Whenever a client leaves my surgery, I give thanks. It only takes a second but, I feel good when I do.

This doesn't mean that we have to be constantly saying 'thank you', but it does mean that we could become more aware of, no only the good things in our lives, but also the not-so-good things.

When it comes to *Gratitude* I use the following questions:

WHY – Why should I say 'thank you' ?

Whenever I do something for someone, I like to be thanked for it. It is not my ego that requires thanks, but it is my self-respect and self-esteem that responds to thanks. It makes me feel good. I would assume that everyone feels good when they are thanked for something they have done. You send 'Thank You' cards to your friends all the time. You feel good when you receive them – as do your friends. You, very simply, 'feel good'.

So, if there is a supreme power / being / force that has the ability to manifest all sorts of goodies into our life, I think that it is only polite and respectful to say 'Thank You'. I'll bet he / she / it will 'feel good'

102

(or should that be 'feel **God**')- when gratitude is expressed.

WHO – Who do I thank ?

The truth is - I'm not sure. Do we say 'thank you' to one being for everything, or do we thank a range of beings ? Beings like: the nature spirits; God; The Universe; Angels or Guides. In essence, it doesn't actually matter who you thank.

The main point is - we receive everything in our lives from an unknown source. Whether we do this alone, or whether we get help – we have no concrete evidence.

Let's assume for a moment that we do this alone. Let's assume that we are almighty and can produce/ create everything ourselves and there is no one else out there. So, when we say 'Thank You', we are thanking ourselves. There's no harm in that.

But, on the other hand, if there is another being involved in creating our wealth, health etc., then I feel that it is only polite and respectful to thank that being.

As human beings, I believe that we are not capable of fully understanding how the universe works. Our scientists believe that they are getting very close to explaining the origins of the universe. They are getting closer to knowing when and how the big bang occurred. To me, that is amazing. My only question is: "what was going on *before* the big bang??". And more (or less) importantly, what was going on before that ??

I know that it is a human desire to understand everything about where we came from, and why we are here, but I believe that we are not capable of fully understanding all of this. I believe it is the arrogance of man that drives us on and on towards knowing everything. It seems to me that the more questions we answer, the more questions appear.

Have you noticed whenever they 'discover' a new fact about our origins, within days or weeks someone else 'discovers' the opposite – or another different fact which contradicts the first one.

Global warming was caused by the Ozone layer breaking up – now it is cows flatulence !

Remember when the world was flat ??

Remember when the moon was made from cheese??

Remember when space was a vacuum – now there is something there ?

Remember when we 'knew' that dinosaurs and humans lived in different eras ? – now we are not sure.

These findings are constantly being corrected and updated.

To fully understand how the Laws of the Universe work is an ongoing lesson, and a lesson that we may *never* fully grasp.

You may not always get what you want,

But, you will always get what you need.

It is worth noting that not all of our 'wants' are met.

Depending on your religious beliefs, your experience of life or your philosophy on the origins of the universe, you must acknowledge that all of your needs *are* met, and you are not always the one to produce those needs. So, they must be guided to you from some other source. You can call that source whatever you like.

Everybody likes to be appreciated for whatever they do. The men who empty your rubbish bin, the shopkeeper, the flight attendant, even your spouse or partner (Wow!! - what a concept !!)

When you show your appreciation and say 'thank you', you are simply acknowledging the fact that:

- This person exists in your world.

- This person has gone to some (or a lot of) trouble to serve you in some way.

- This person or item has turned up in your life at your time of need.

So, when you say 'thank you' to the universe for something, you are simply acknowledging:

- it's existence.

- the trouble it has gone to - for you.

- that it has turned up at the right time.

Learn to say 'thank you' for everything – the good and the bad. It is always easy to say 'thank you' for the 'good things', but why would you want to say 'thank you' for the 'bad things' ?

The reason is this. What appears to be a 'bad thing' at first, may not end up being a bad thing. To me, everything is a lesson. I believe that the bad things have more powerful lessons than the lessons we learn from the good things.

> **You can have a 'bad' experience**
>
> **but**
>
> **no experience is ever bad for you**

WHEN – When should I do it ? Everyday – or more specifically, every night.

Every night, as you turn out the light to go to sleep, spend a moment reflecting on the day. This day will never come again. Take a mental note of the events of the day. Who did you meet during the day ? How did these events and people effect your feelings, and, more importantly, what you have learned from the day? You can miss out on endless opportunities and lessons if you don't do this.

When you have reflected on the day – say 'Thank You' for the experience – and, of course, the lesson. At this point in your life, it doesn't actually matter if you understand the lesson.

By doing this little exercise, you will become more conscious / aware of more and more seemingly insignificant happenings throughout your day.

WHERE – Where should I do it ? As I have suggested, do it the last thing at night.

I give thanks at the end of a workshop - as I drive home.

I give thanks when a client leaves my surgery. I give thanks whenever I think of it. It will never do any harm – and it makes me more conscious of the quality of my life. I am constantly aware of the many blessings I have in my life.

HOW – How do I do it ? It is not necessary to get down on your knees at the side of your bed in order to give thanks. You can do it anywhere. However, as I have suggested above, at least once a day, take a particular time and place to give thanks – in bed, last thing at night for example. It makes it a formal ritual and more profound.

In your mind, just reflect and say 'THANK YOU'.

Of course, I'm sure that you can think of ways and times that might suit you better. It doesn't matter – just as long as you remember to give thanks.

Conclusion

And there you have it. A lot of information to absorb and put into practise. But, as I said at the beginning, be: open minded, committed, disciplined and eager to learn.

As you practise these techniques regularly, you will find that your life begins to 'feel' different. You may notice small changes at first. You may notice that you are in a better frame of mind. Your attitude towards your work, your responsibilities, your health, your finances and many other parts of your life becomes more positive.

We all have our ups and downs. But now you can have more control over the downs, which leaves more room for the ups.

To me, it all comes down to 'awareness'.

The more aware we are, the more control we have.

The more control we have, the more secure and safe we feel.

The more secure we feel, the happier and more contented we become.

And that is what it is all about – being happy and contented.

Conclusion

The problems we encounter as we go through our life can become challenges.

By using the suggestions from this little book, you can turn a negative situation (a problem) into a challenge.

When you watch participants on a TV game show being challenged to a task, what thoughts go through your head. Are they thoughts of - "they'll never be able to do that" – or "this is a huge problem to overcome". No, I would imagine that your thoughts are something like "go on – you can do it" or "keep going – keep going, you can do it!"

We can get very excited when watch others overcome obstacles on the television. How excited could you become when you look at the 'obstacles' in your own life?

Just imagine a problem you are experiencing right now in your life. Imagine your were a participant on a TV show and were asked to solve the problem. How would you behave?? Would you:

- Sit down and moan about how difficult it is ?

- Look to someone else to solve the problem ?

- Give up without even trying ?

I don't think so ! You would be up there battling away and enjoying the challenge. Your attitude would be positive and energetic. I would imagine that you would overcome the challenge quite easily – and feel great.

So, why not adopt this attitude with every 'problem' in your life – starting from today.

It is all in your mind. Your attitudes, your motivation and your ability to solve issues. They are all yours to implement, whenever you choose.

This book is not just about following the instructions and being happy. It is about discovering what parts of this book work for you, making up your own mind to make positive changes and then put these changes into action.

That's the secret – **just do it.**

You can read as many books as you like. You can attend as many motivational seminars as you can fit into your spare time but – none of them will change your life until you **take action**.

Choose today to adopt this new approach and start making major changes in your life.

Good luck - and may your 'God' bless you.

111

Many Thanks

As I have stated at the beginning of this book, I re-educated myself to become the kind of person whom I like – and dare I say it – love.

By learning to love myself more, I have become more aware of the times in the past when I gave away my power to others.

There are many people to thank for my re-education. This re-education took the shape of training courses, articles in journals, CDs and tapes, books by spiritual masters and teachers, business articles, comments from well meaning friends and colleagues, networking with high level successful business people and more.

Since I have become more aware, I have 'soaked in' information and teachings like a sponge.

Some of these I wish to thank are:

Dr. Wayne Dyer

Anthony Robbins

Dr. David Hamilton

Louise L. Hay

Many Thanks

Lynne McTaggart

Esther & Jerry Hicks

Neale Donald Walsche

Patricia Iris Kerins – my lovely wife and best friend

And there are lots more

To these beautiful, enlightened people I say a big

Thank You

You have helped change my life.

Biography

Bill Kerins was born and raised in Dublin, Ireland. Upon leaving school, he served an apprenticeship and worked in Aircraft Engineering until 1982 when he decided that he was a 'people' person and not a 'things' person.

He retrained as a Training Consultant and ran his own very successful training company helping unemployed youth and women returning to work.

He immigrated to Oxford in England in 1989, worked as a training consultant with unemployed and disabled people for three years, until he moved his family to the Highlands of Scotland, where he built his own house in the countryside over a three year period.

In 2001, he embarked on a new venture to re-educate himself and become a Hypnotherapist, Meridian Therapist and Life Coach. Since then he has formed his own school of Hypnotherapy called **'The Kerinsian School of Hypnotherapy & EFT'.**

He calls his approach to his work 'The Kerinsian Approach'. This approach incorporates all of the various learning and life experiences he has had throughout his life, which makes it unique in itself.

115

Biography

His aim in life is to help people to wake up, step into their own power, to recognise and become the person they really are.

He is the father of four wonderful grown up adults and grandfather of five grandchildren.

He spends his working time with private consultations, corporate training, teaching, supervising Hypnotherapists, writing and speaking at various events.

At present, he lives in the central belt of Scotland with his wife Patricia Iris Kerins.

Email Bill on: bill@billkerins.com

www.billkerins.com

Are you interested in learning more about

The Kerinsian Keys ?

For details of workshops and courses please visit the website at:

www.billkerins.com

or contact me on:

bill@billkerins.com

I also run training courses in:

Hypnotherapy Diploma Courses
accredited by
The National Council for Hypnotherapists (NCH)

E.F.T. (Emotional Freedom Techniques)
accredited by
The Association for the Advancement of Meridian
Energy Therapies (AAMET)

Bill is a certified board member and instructor for
The National Guild of Hypnotists (USA).

Notes